The Crescent Moon Book of Elizabethan Love Poetry

Edited by Carol Appleby

CRESCENT MOON

CRESCENT MOON PUBLISHING
P.O. Box 1312, Maidstone
Kent, ME14 5XU
United Kingdom

First published 1999. Second edition 2008. Pocket edition
2022.
Introduction © Carol Appleby, 1999, 2008, 2022.

Set in Times New Roman 9 on 12 pt.
Designed by Radiance Graphics.

British Library Cataloguing in Publication data available

The Crescent Moon Book of Elizabethan Love Poetry.
(British Poets Series)
1. Love poetry, English 2. English poetry – Early modern,
1500-1700
I. Appleby, Carol

821.3'08'03543

ISBN-13 9781861711359
ISBN-13 9781861718471

POETRY FROM CRESCENT
MOON

Walking In Cornwall
by Ursula Le Guin

Hymns To the Night
by Novalis

*Hymns To the Night: In
Translation*
by Novalis

*Flower Pollen: Selected
Thoughts*
by Novalis

*Novalis: His Life, Thoughts
and Works*
by Novalis

Edmund Spenser: *Heavenly
Love: Selected Poems*
selected and introduced by
Teresa Page

Edmund Spenser: *Amoretti*
edited by Teresa Page

*The Visions of Petrarch and
Bellay: Early Sonnets*
by Edmund Spenser

Percy Bysshe Shelley:
*Paradise of Golden Lights:
Selected Poems*
selected and introduced by
Charlotte Greene

Robert Herrick: *Delight In
Disorder: Selected Poems*
edited and introduced by
M.K. Pace

Robert Herrick: *Hesperides*
edited and introduced by
M.K. Pace

Robert Herrick: *Upon Julia's
Breasts: Love Poems*
edited and introduced by
M.K. Pace

Sir Thomas Wyatt: *Love For
Love: Selected Poems*
selected and introduced by
Louise Cooper

John Donne: *Air and Angels:
Selected Poems*
selected and introduced by
A.H. Ninham

D.H. Lawrence: *Being Alive:
Selected Poems*
edited with an introduction by
Margaret Elvy

D.H. Lawrence: *Amores*
edited with an introduction by
Margaret Elvy

D.H. Lawrence: *Look! We
Have Come Through!*
edited with an introduction by
Margaret Elvy

D.H. Lawrence: *Love Poems and Others*
edited with an introduction by Margaret Elvy

D.H. Lawrence: *New Poems*
edited with an introduction by Margaret Elvy

D.H. Lawrence: Symbolic Landscapes
by Jane Foster

D.H. Lawrence: Infinite Sensual Violence
by M.K. Pace

Thomas Hardy: *Her Haunting Ground: Selected Poems*
edited, with an introduction by A.H. Ninham

Thomas Hardy: *Late Lyrics and Earlier*
edited, with an introduction by A.H. Ninham

Thomas Hardy: *Moments of Vision*
edited, with an introduction by A.H. Ninham

Thomas Hardy: *Poems of the Past and the Present*
edited, with an introduction by A.H. Ninham

Thomas Hardy: *Satires of Circumstance*
edited, with an introduction by A.H. Ninham

Thomas Hardy: *Time's Laughingstocks*
edited, with an introduction by A.H. Ninham

Thomas Hardy: *Wessex Poems*
edited, with an introduction by A.H. Ninham

Sexing Hardy: Thomas Hardy and Feminism
by Margaret Elvy

Emily Bronte: *Darkness and Glory: Selected Poems*
selected and introduced by Miriam Chalk

John Keats: *Bright Star: Selected Poems*
edited with an introduction by Miriam Chalk

John Keats: *Poems of 1820*
edited with an introduction by Miriam Chalk

Henry Vaughan: *A Great Ring of Pure and Endless Light: Selected Poems*
selected and introduced by A.H. Ninham

Arthur Rimbaud: *Selected Poems*
edited and translated by
Andrew Jary

Arthur Rimbaud: *A Season in Hell*
edited and translated by
Andrew Jary

Canzoniere
by Francesco Petrarch

Friedrich Hölderlin:
Hölderlin's Songs of Light: Selected Poems
translated by Michael Hamburger

Rainer Maria Rilke: *Dance the Orange: Selected Poems*
translated by Michael Hamburger

Rainer Maria Rilke: *Poems*
translated by Jessie Lamont

Auguste Rodin
by Rainer Maria Rilke

Rilke: Space, Essence and Angels In the Poetry of Rainer Maria Rilke
by B.D. Barnacle

German Romantic Poetry: Goethe, Novalis, Heine, Hölderlin
by Carol Appleby

The North Sea
by Heinrich Heine

Rampoli: Poems From Mainly German
by George Macdonald

Arseny Tarkovsky: *Life, Life: Selected Poems*
translated by Virginia Rounding

Emily Dickinson: *Wild Nights: Selected Poems*
selected by Miriam Chalk

Delia
by Samuel Daniel

Idea
by Michael Drayton

Astrophil and Stella
by Sir Philip Sidney

Elizabethan Sonnet Cycles
by Daniel, Drayton, Sidney, Spenser and Shakespeare

Elizabethan Sonnet Cycles
(Volume Two)
by Lodge, Griffin, Smith, Constable and Fletcher

Three Metaphysical Poets
edited by A.H. Ninham

Three Romantic Poets
edited by Miriam Chalk

The Crescent Moon Book
of Elizabethan Love Poetry

Contents

QUEEN ELIZABETH I

(1533-1603)

On Monsieur's Departure

I GRIEVE and dare not show my discontent,
I love and yet am forced to seem to hate,
I do, yet dare not say I ever meant,
I seem stark mute but inwardly do pate.
    I am and am not, I freeze and yet am burned,
    Since from myself another self I turned.

My care is like my shadow in the sun,
Follows me flying, flies when I pursue it,
Stands and lies by me, doth what I have done.
His too familiar care doth make me rue it.
    No means I find to rid him from my breast,
    Till by the end of things it be suppressed.

Some gentler passion slide into my mind,
For I am soft and made of melting snow;
Or be more cruel, love, and so be kind.
Let me float or sink, be high or low.
    Or let me live with some more sweet content,
    Or die and so forget what love e'er meant.

EDWARD DE VERE,
EARL OF OXFORD
(1550-1604)

"What cunning can express"

WHAT CUNNING can express
    The favour of her face,
To whom in this distress
    I do appeal for grace.
        A thousand Cupids fly
        About her gentle eye.

From whence each throws a dart
    That kindleth soft sweet fire
Within my sighing heart,
    Possessed by desire.
        No sweeter life I try
        Than in her love to die.

The lily in the field,
    That glories in his white,
For pureness now must yield
    And render up his right.

Heaven pictured in her face
Doth promise joy and grace.

Fair Cynthia's silver light,
That beats on running stream
Compares not with her white,
Whose hairs are all sunbeams.
Her virtues so do shine,
As day unto mine eyne.

With this there is a red
Exceeds the damask rose,
Which in her cheeks is spread,
Whence every favour grows.
In sky there is nos tar,
That she surmounts not far.

When Phoebus from the bed
Of Thetis doth arise,
The morning blushing red
In fair carnation wise,
He shows it in her face,
As queen of every grace.

This pleasant lily white,
This taint of roseate red,
This Cynthia's silver light,
This sweet fair Dea spread

These sunbeams in mine eye;
These beauties make me die.

SIR WALTER RALEIGH
(*c.* 1557-1618)

The Nymph's Reply to the Sheepheard

IF ALL the world and love were young,
And truth in every Sheepheard's tongue,
These pretty pleasures might me move,
To live with thee, and be thy love.

Time drives the flocks from field to fold,
When Rivers rage, and rocks grow cold,
And Philomell becometh dombe,
The rest complaines of cares to come.

The flowers do fade, and wanton fieldes,
To wayward winter reckoning yeeldes,
A honny tongue, a hart of gall,
Is fancies spring, but sorrowes fall.

Thy gownes, thy shooes, thy beds of Roses,
Thy cap, thy kirtle, and thy poesies,
Soone breake, soone wither, soone forgotten:
In follie ripe, in reason rotten.

Thy belt of straw and ivie buddes,
Thy Corall claspes and Amber studdes,
All these in me no meanes can move,
To come to thee, and be they love.

But could youth last, and love still breede,
Had joyes no date, nor age no neede,
Then these delights my minde might move,
To live with thee, and by thy love.

EDMUND SPENSER
(*c.* 1552-1599)

from *Amoretti*

3

THE SOUVERAYNE beauty which I do admyre,
    witnesse the world how worthy to be
                    prayzed:
    the light whereof hath kindled heavenly fyre,
    in my fraile spirit by her from basenesse
                    raysed.
That being now with her huge brightnesse dazed,
    base thing I can no more endure to view:
    but looking still on her I stand amazed,
    at wondrous sight of so celestial hew.
So when my tongue would speak her praises dew,
    it stopped is with thoughts astonishment:
    and when my pen would write her titles true,
    it ravisht is with fancies wonderment:
Yet in my heart I then both speake and write
    the wonder that my wit cannot endite.

8

MORE THEN most faire, full of the living fire,
    kindled above unto the maker neare:
    no eyes but joyes, in which all powers
                conspire,
    that to the world naught else be counted
                deare.
Through your bright beames doth not the
                blinded guest,
    shoot out his darts to base affections wound:
    but angels come to lead fraile mindes to rest
    in chaste desires on heavenly beauty bound.
You frame my thoughts and fashion my within,
    you stop my tongue, and teach my hart to
                speake,
    you calme the torme that passion did begin,
    strong through your cause, but by your
                virtue weak.
Dark is the world, where your light shined never;
    well is he borne, that may behold you ever.

THE GLORIOUS portrait of that Angels face,
    Made to amaze weake mens confused skil:
    and this worlds worthlesse glory to embase,
    what pen, what pencill can expresse her fill?
For though he colours could deuize at will,
    and eke his learned hand at pleasure guide:
    least trembling it his wormanship should
              spill,
    yet many wondrous things there are beside.
The sweet eye-glaunces, that like arrowes glide,
    the charming smiles, that rob sence from the
              hart:
    the louely pleasance and the lofty pride,
    cannot expressed be by any art.
A greater craftesmans hand thereto doth neede,
    that can expresse the life of things indeed.

THIS HOLY season fit to fast and pray,
    men to devotion ought to be inclind:
    therefore, I likewise on so holy day,
    for my sweet Saint some service fit will find.
Her temple faire is built within my mind,
    in which her glorious image placed is,
    on which my thoughts do day and night
                    attend
    like sacred priests that never thinke amisse.
There I to her as th'author of my blise,
    will builde an altar to appease her ire:
    and on the same my hart will sacrifice,
    burning in flames of pure and chast desire:
The which vouchsafe O goddesse to accept,
    amongst thy dearest relicks to be kept.

SWEET SMILE, the daughter of the Queene of
               love,
    expressing all thy mothers powerful art:
    with which she wonts to temper angry love,
    when all the gods he threats with thundring
               dart.
Sweet is thy virtue as thyselfe sweet art,
    for when on me thou shinedst late in
               sadnesse,
    a melting pleasance ran through every part,
    and me revived with heart robbing
               gladnesse.
Whilest rapt with joy resembling heavenly
               madnesse,
    my soule was ravisht quite as in a trance:
    and feeling thence no more her sorrowes
               sadnesse,
    fed on the fulnesse of that cheerful glance,
More sweet than Nectar or Ambrosial meat,
    seemed every bit, which thenceforth I did eat.

COMING TO kisse her lips, (such grace I found)
    me seemed I smelt a garden of sweet flowers:
    that dainty odours from them threw around
    for damzels fit to decke their lovers bowers.
Her lips did smell like unto Gillyflowers,
    her ruddy cheekes like unto Roses red:
    her snowy brows like budded Bellamoures,
    her lovely eyes like Pinks but newly spread.
Her goodly bosome like a Strawberry bed,
    her neck like to a bunch of Columbines:
    her brest like lillies, ere their leaves be shed,
    her nipples like young blossomed
                    Jessemines.
Such fragrant flowres do give most odorous
                 smell,
    but her sweet odour did them all excell.

FAIRE BOSOME fraught with virtues richest
>> treasure,
> the neast of love, the lodging of delight:
> the bowre of blisse, the paradise of pleasure,
> the sacred harbour of that heavenly spright.
How was I ravisht with your lovely sight,
> and my fraile thoughts too rashly led astray?
> whiles diving deepe through amorous
>> insight,
> on the sweet spoile of beautie they did pray.
And twixt her paps like early fruit in May.
> whose harvest seemed to hasten now apace:
> they loosely did their wanton winges
>> display,
>> and there to rest themselves did boldly
>>> place.
Sweet thoughts I envy your so happy rest,
> which oft I wisht, yet never as so blest.

from *A Hymn In Honour of Love*

FOR LOVE is Lord of truth and loyaltie,
Lifting himselfe out of the lowly dust,
On golden plumes up to the purest skie,
Above the reach of loathly sinfull lust,
Whose base affect through cowardly distrust
Of his weake wings, dare not to heaven fly,
But like a moldwarpe in the earth doth ly.

His dunghill thoughts, which do themselves
                       enure
To dirtie drosse, no higher dare aspire,
Ne can his feeble earthly eyes endure
The flaming light of that celestiall desire,
And makes him mount above the native might
Of heavie earth, up to the heavens light.

Such is the powre of that sweet passion,
That it all sordid basenesse doth expell,
And the refined mind doth newly fashion
Unto a fairer forme, which now doth dwell
In his high thought, that would itselfe excell;
Which he beholding still with constant sight,
Admires the mirrour of so heavenly light.

Whose image printing in his deepest wit,

He thereon feeds his hungrie fantasy,
Still full, yet never satisfyde with it,
Like Tantale, that in store doth sterued ly:
So doth he pine in most satiety,
For nought may quench his infinite desire,
Once kindled through that first conceived fire.

Epithalamion

Ye learned Sisters, which have oftentimes
Beene to me ayding, others to adorne
Whom ye thought worthy of your gracefull
                                                          rymes,
That even the greatest did not greatly scorne
To heare theyr names sung in your simple layes,
But ioyed in theyr praise,
And when ye list your own mishaps to mourne,
Which death, or love, or fortunes wreck did rayse,
Your string could soone to sadder tenor turne,
And teach the woods and waters to lament
Your dolefull dreriment,
Now lay those sorrowfull complaints aside,
And having all your heads with girlands crownd,
Helpe me mine owne Loves prayses to resound:
Ne let the same of any be envide:
So Orpheus did for his owne bride;
So I unto my selfe alone will sing;
The woods shall to me answer, and my eccho ring.

Early, before the worlds light-giving lampe
His golden beame upon the hils doth spred,
Having disperst the nights unchearfull dampe,
Doe ye awake, and, with fresh lustyhed,
Go to the bowre of my beloved Love,

My truest turtle dove.
Bid her awake; for Hymen is awake,
And long since ready forth his maske to move,
With his bright tead that flames with many a
flake,
And many a bachelor to waite on him,
In theyr fresh garments trim.
Bid her awake therefore, and soone her dight,
For loe! the wished day is come at last,
That shall for all the paynes and sorrowes past
Pay to her usury of long delight:
And whylest she doth her dight,
Doe ye to her of ioy and solace sing,
That all the woods may answer, and your eccho
ring.

Bring with you all the nymphes that you can
heare,
Both of the rivers and the forrests greene,
And of the sea that neighbours to her neare,
All with gay girlands goodly wel beseene.
And let them also with them bring in hand
Another gay girland,
For my fayre Love, of lillyes and of roses,
Bound truelove wize with a blew silke riband.
And let them make great store of bridale poses,
And let them eke bring store of other flowers,
To deck the bridale bowers:

And let the ground whereas her foot shall tread,
For feare the stones her tender foot should wrong,
Be strewd with fragrant flowers all along,
And diapred lyke the discolored mead.
Which done, doe at her chamber dore awayt,
For she will waken strayt;
The whiles do ye this song unto her sing,
The woods shall to you answer, and your eccho
                         ring.

Ye Nymphes of Mulla, which with carefull heed
The silver scaly trouts do tend full well,
And greedy pikes which use therein to feed,
(Those trouts and pikes all others doe excell,)
And ye likewise which keepe the rushy lake,
Where none doo fishes take,
Bynd up the locks the which hang scatterd light,
And in his waters, which your mirror make,
Behold your faces as the christall bright,
That when you come whereas my Love doth lie,
No blemish she may spie.
And eke, ye lightfoot mayds which keepe the dere
That on the hoary mountayne use to towre,
And the wylde wolves, which seeke them to
                         devoure,
With your steele darts doe chace from coming
                         neer,
Be also present heere,

To helpe to decke her, and to help to sing,
That all the woods may answer, and your eccho
                                        ring.

Wake now, my Love, awake! for it is time:
The rosy Morne long since left Tithons bed,
All ready to her silver coche to clyme,
And Phoebus gins to shew his glorious hed.
Hark! how the cheerefull birds do chaunt theyr
                                        laies,
And carroll of Loves praise:
The merry larke hir mattins sings aloft;
The thrush replyes; the mavis descant playes;
The ouzell shrills; the ruddock warbles soft;
So goodly all agree, with sweet consent,
To this dayes meriment.
Ah! my deere Love, why doe ye sleepe thus long,
When meeter were that ye should now awake,
T'away the comming of your ioyous make,
And hearken to the birds love-learned song,
The deawy leaves among!
For they of ioy and pleasance to you sing,
That all the woods them answer, and theyr eccho
                                        ring.

My love is now awake out of her dreame,
And her fayre eyes, like stars that dimmed were
With darksome cloud, now shew theyr goodly

beams

More bright then Hesperus his head doth rere.
Come now, ye damzels, daughters of delight,
Helpe quickly her to dight.
But first come, ye fayre Houres, which were begot,
In Ioves sweet paradice, of Day and Night,
Which doe the seasons of the year allot,
And all that ever in this world is fayre
Do make and still repayre:
And ye three handmayds of the Cyprian Queene,
The which doe still adorn her beauties pride,
Helpe to adorne my beautifullest bride:
And, as ye her array, still throw betweene
Some graces to be scene;
And, as ye use to Venus, to her sing,
The whiles the woods shal answer, and your
eccho ring.

Now is my Love all ready forth to come:
Let all the virgins therefore well awayt,
And ye fresh boyes, that tend upon her groome,
Prepare your selves, for he is comming strayt.
Set all your things in seemely good aray,
Fit for so ioyfull day,
The ioyfulst day that ever sunne did see.
Fair Sun! shew forth thy favourable ray,
And let thy lifull heat not fervent be,
For feare of burning her sunshyny face,

Her beauty to disgrace.
O fayrest Phoebus! Father of the Muse!
If ever I did honour thee aright,
Or sing the thing that mote thy mind delight,
Doe not thy servants simple boone refuse,
But let this day, let this one day, be mine;
Let all the rest be thine.
Then I thy soverayne prayses loud wil sing,
That all the woods shal answer, and theyr eccho
                       ring.

Harke! how the minstrils gin to shrill aloud
Their merry musick that resounds from far,
The pipe, the tabor, and the trembling croud,
That well agree withouten breach or iar.
But most of all the damzels doe delite,
When they their tymbrels smyte,
And thereunto doe daunce and carrol sweet,
That all the sences they doe ravish quite;
The whyles the boyes run up and downe the
                       street,
Crying aloud with strong confused noyce,
As if it were one voyce,
'Hymen, Ioe Hymen, Hymen,' they do shout;
That even to the heavens theyr shouting shrill
Doth reach, and all the firmament doth fill;
To which the people, standing all about,
As in approvance, doe thereto applaud,

And loud advaunce her laud;
And evermore they 'Hymen, Hymen,' sing,
That all the woods them answer, and theyr eccho
                                    ring.

Loe! where she comes along with portly pace,
Lyke Phoebe, from her chamber of the East,
Arysing forth to run her mighty race,
Clad all in white, that seems a virgin best.
So well it her beseems, that ye would weene
Some angell she had beene.
Her long loose yellow locks lyke golden wyre,
Sprinckled with perle, and perling flowres
                                    atweene,
Doe lyke a golden mantle her attyre,
And, being crowned with a girland greene,
Seem lyke some mayden queene.
Her modest eyes, abashed to behold
So many gazers as on her do stare,
Upon the lowly ground affixed are,
Ne dare lift up her countenance too bold,
But blush to heare her prayses sung so loud,–
So farre from being proud.
Nathlesse doe ye still loud her prayses sing,
That all the woods may answer, and your eccho
                                    ring.

Tell me, ye merchants daughters, did ye see

So fayre a creature in your towne before;
So sweet, so lovely, and so mild as she,
Adornd with beautyes grace and vertues store?
Her goodly eyes lyke saphyres shining bright,
Her forehead yvory white,
Her cheekes lyke apples which the sun hath
rudded,
Her lips lyke cherries, charming men to byte,
Her brest like to a bowl of creame uncrudded,
Her paps lyke lyllies budded,
Her snowie necke lyke to a marble towre,
And all her body like a pallace fayre,
Ascending up, with many a stately stayre,
To honors seat and chastities sweet bowre.
Why stand ye still, ye virgins, in amaze,
Upon her so to gaze,
Whiles ye forget your former lay to sing,
To which the woods did answer, and your eccho
ring?

But if ye saw that which no eyes can see,
The inward beauty of her lively spright,
Garnisht with heavenly guifts of high degree,
Much more then would ye wonder at that sight,
And stand astonisht lyke to those which red
Medusaes mazeful hed.
There dwells sweet Love, and constant Chastity,
Unspotted Fayth, and comely Womanhood,

Regard of Honour, and mild Modesty;
There Vertue raynes as quecne in royal throne,
And giveth lawes alone,
The which the base affections doe obay,
And yeeld theyr services unto her will;
Be thought of tilings uncomely ever may
Thereto approch to tempt her mind to ill.
Had ye once seene these her celestial threasures,
And unrevealed pleasures,
Then would ye wonder, and her prayses sing,
That all the woods should answer, and your eccho
ring.

Open the temple gates unto my Love,
Open them wide that she may enter in,
And all the postes adorne as doth behove,
And all the pillours deck with girlands trim,
For to receyve this saynt with honour dew,
That commeth in to you.
With trembling steps and humble reverence,
She commeth in before th'Almighties view:
Of her, ye virgins, learne obedience,
When so ye come into those holy places,
To humble your proud faces.
Bring her up to th'high altar, that she may
The sacred ceremonies there partake,
The which do endlesse matrimony make;
And let the roring organs loudly play

The praises of the Loi'd in lively notes;
The whiles, with hollow throates,
The choristers the ioyous antheme sing,
That all the woods may answer, and their eccho
                              ring.

Behold, whiles she before the altar stands,
Hearing the holy priest that to her speakes
And blesseth her with his two happy hands,
How the red roses flush up in her cheekes,
And the pure snow with goodly vermill stayne,
Like crimsin dyde in grayne:
That even the angels, which continually
About the sacred altar doe remaine,
Forget their service and about her fly,
Ofte peeping in her face, that seems more fayre
The more they on it stare.
But her sad eyes, still fastened on the ground,
Are governed with goodly modesty,
That suffers not one look to glaunce awry,
Which may let in a little thought unsownd.
Why blush ye, Love, to give to me your hand,
The pledge of all our band?
Sing, ye sweet angels, Alleluya sing,
That all the woods may answer, and your eccho
                              ring.

Now al is done; bring home the bride againe;

Bring home the triumph of our victory;
Bring home with you the glory of her game,
With ioyance bring her and with iollity.
Never had man more ioyfull day than this,
Whom heaven would heape with blis.
Make feast therefore now all this live-long day;
This day for ever to me holy is.
Poure out the wine without restraint or stay,
Poure not by cups, but by the belly full,
Poure out to all that wull,
And sprinkle all the posts and wals with wine,
That they may sweat, and drunken be withall.
Crowne ye god Bacchus with a coronall,
And Hymen also crowne with wreaths of vine;
And let the Graces daunce unto the rest,
For they can doo it best:
The whiles the maydens doe theyr carroll sing,
To which the woods shall answer, and theyr eccho
ring.

Ring ye the bels, ye yong men of the towne,
And leave your wonted labors for this day:
This day is holy; doe ye write it downe,
That ye for ever it remember may.
This day the sunne is in his chiefest hight,
With Barnaby the bright,
From whence declining daily by degrees,
He somewhat loseth of his heat and light,

When once the Crab behind his back he sees.
But for this time it ill ordained was,
To choose the longest day in all the yeare,
And shortest night, when longest fitter weare:
Yet never day so long, but late would passe.
Ring ye the bels to make it weare away,
And bonefiers make all day;
And daunce about them, and about them sing,
That all the woods may answer, and your eccho
                                        ring.

Ah! when will this long weary day have end,
And lende me leave to come unto my Love?
How slowly do the houres theyr numbers spend?
How slowly does sad Time his feathers move?
Hast thee, O fayrest planet, to thy home,
Within the Westerne fome:
Thy tyred steedes long since have need of rest.
Long though it be, at last I see it gloome,
And the bright evening-star with golden creast
Appeare out of the East.
Fayre childe of beauty! glorious lampe of love!
That all the host of heaven in rankes doost lead,
And guidest lovers through the nights sad dread,
How chearefully thou lookest from above,
And seemst to laugh atweene thy twinkling light,
As ioying in the sight
Of these glad many, which for ioy do sing,

That all the woods them answer, and their eccho
                    ring!

Now ceasse, ye damsels, your delights fore-past;
Enough it is that all the day was youres:
Now day is doen, and night is nighing fast;
Now bring the bryde into the brydall bowres.
The night is come; now soon her disaray,
And in her bed her lay;
Lay her in lillies and in violets,
And silken curteins over her display,
And odourd sheets, and Arras coverlets.
Behold how goodly my faire Love does ly,
In proud humility!
Like unto Maia, when as Iove her took
In Tempe, lying on the flowry gras,
Twixt sleepe and wake, after she weary was
With bathing in the Acidalian brooke.
Now it is night, ye damsels may be gone,
And leave my Love alone,
And leave likewise your former lay to sing:
The woods no more shall answer, nor your eccho
                    ring.

Now welcome, Night! thou night so long
                    expected,
That long daies labour doest at last defray,
And all my cares, which cruell Love collected,

Hast sumd in one, and cancelled for aye.
Spread thy broad wing over my Love and me,
That no man may us see;
And in thy sable mantle us enwrap,
From feare of perrill and foule horror free.
Let no false treason seeke us to entrap,
Nor any dread disquiet once annoy
The safety of our ioy;
But let the night be calme and quietsome,
Without tempestuous storms or sad afray;
Lyke as when Ioue with fayre Alemena lay,
When he begot the great Tirynthian groome;
Or lyke as when he with thy selfe did lie,
And begot Maiesty:
And let the mayds and yongmen cease to sing;
Ne let the woods them answer, nor theyr eccho
                              ring.

Let no lamenting cryes, nor dolefull teares,
Be heard all night within, nor yet without:
Ne let false whispers, breeding hidden feares,
Breake gentle sleepe with misconceived dout.
Let no deluding dreames, nor dreadful sights,
Make sudden sad affrights:
No let house-fyres, nor lightnings helpless
                              harmes,
Ne let the Pouke, nor other evill sprights,
Ne let mischievous witches with theyr charmes,

Ne let hob-goblins, names whose sence we see
                                    not,
Fray us with things that be not:
Let not the shriech-owle, nor the storke, be heard,
Nor the night-raven, that still deadly yels,
Nor damned ghosts, cald up with mighty spels,
Nor griesly vultures, make us once affeard:
Ne let th'unpleasant quyre of frogs still croking
Make us to wish theyr choking.
Let none of these theyr drery accents sing;
Ne let the woods them answer, nor theyr eccho
                                    ring.

But let stil Silence trew night-watches keepe,
That sacred Peace may in assurance rayne,
And tymely Sleep, when it is tyme to sleepe,
May poure his limbs forth on your pleasant
                                    playne.
The whiles an hundred little winged Loves,
Like divers-fethered doves,
Shall fly and flutter round about the bed,
And in the secret darke, that none reproves,
Their prety stealthes shall worke, and snares shall
                                    spread
To filch away sweet snatches of delight,
Conceald through covert night.
Ye sonnes of Venus, play your sports at will!
For greedy Pleasure, carelesse of your toyes,

Thinks more upon her paradise of ioyes,
Then what ye do, albe it good or ill.
All night, therefore, attend your merry play,
For it will soone be day:
Now none doth hinder you, that say or sing;
Ne will the woods now answer, nor your eccho
ring.

Who is the same which at my window peepes?
Or whose is that faire face that shines so bright?
Is it not Cinthia, she that never sleepes,
But walkes about high heaven al the night?
O fayrest goddesse! do thou not envy
My Love with me to spy:
For thou likewise didst love, though now
unthought,
And for a fleece of wooll, which privily
The Latmian Shepherd once unto thee brought,
His pleasures with thee wrought.
Therefore to us be favorable now;
And sith of wemens labours thou hast charge,
And generation goodly dost enlarge,
Encline thy will t'effect our wishfull vow,
And the chast womb informe with timely seed,
That may our comfort breed:
Till which we cease our hopefull hap to sing,
Ne let the woods us answer, nor our eccho ring.

And thou, great Juno! which with awful might
The lawes of wedlock still dost patronize,
And the religion of the faith first plight
With sacred rites hast taught to solemnize,
And eke for comfort often called art
Of women in their smart,
Eternally bind thou this lovely band,
And all thy blessings unto us impart.
And thou, glad Genius! in whose gentle hand
The bridale bowre and geniall bed remaine,
Without blemish or staine,
And the sweet pleasures of theyr loves delight
With secret ayde doost succour and supply,
Till they bring forth the fruitfull progeny,
Send us the timely fruit of this same night,
And thou, fayre Hebe! and thou, Hymen free!
Grant that it may so be.
Till which we cease your further prayse to sing,
Ne any woods shall answer, nor your eccho ring.

And ye high heavens, the temple of the gods,
In which a thousand torches flaming bright
Doe burne, that to us wretched earthly clods
In dreadful darknesse lend desired light,
And all ye powers which in the same remayne,
More than we men can fayne,
Poure out your blessing on us plentiously,
And happy influence upon us raine,

That we may raise a large posterity,
Which from the earth, which they may long
                              possesse
With lasting happinesse,
Up to your haughty pallaces may mount,
And for the guerdon of theyr glorious merit,
May heavenly tabernacles there inherit,
Of blessed saints for to increase the count.
So let us rest, sweet Love, in hope of this,
And cease till then our tymely ioyes to sing:
The woods no more us answer, nor our eccho
                              ring!

Song, made in lieu of many ornaments
With which my Love should duly have been dect,
Which cutting off through hasty accidents,
Ye would not stay your dew time to expect,
But promist both to recompens,
Be unto her a goodly ornament,
And for short time an endlesse moniment!

WILLIAM SMITH

(published 1596)

from *Chloris*

II

Thy beauty subject of my song I make,
O fairest fair, on whom depends my life!
Refuse not then the task I undertake,
To please thy rage and to appease my strife;
But with one smile remunerate my toil,
None other guerdon I of thee desire.
Give not my lowly muse new-hatched the foil,
But warmth that she may at the length aspire
Unto the temples of thy star-bright eyes,
Upon whose round orbs perfect beauty sits,
From whence such glorious crystal beams arise,
As best my Chloris' seemly face befits;
   Which eyes, which beauty, which bright crystal
                    beam,
   Which face of thine hath made my love
                    extreme.

XXII

O fairest fair, to thee I make my plaint,
(my plaint)
To thee from whom my cause of grief doth
spring;
(doth spring)
Attentive be unto the groans, sweet saint,
(sweet saint)
Which unto thee in doleful tunes I sing.
(I sing)
My mournful muse doth always speak of thee;
(of thee)
My love is pure, O do it not disdain!
(disdain)
With bitter sorrow still oppress not me,
(not me)
But mildly look upon me which complain.
(which complain)
Kill not my true-affecting thoughts, but give
(but give)
Such precious balm of comfort to my heart,
(my heart)
That casting off despair in hope to live,
(hope to live)
I may find help at length to ease my smart.
(to ease my smart)

So shall you add such courage to my love,
(my love)
That fortune false my faith shall not remove.
(shall not remove)

XLIII

Thou glorious sun, from whence my lesser light
The substance of his crystal shine doth borrow,
Let these my moans find favour in thy sight.
And with remorse extinguish now my sorrow!
Renew those lamps which thy disdain hath
                              quenched,
As Phœbus doth his sister Phœbe's shine;
Consider how thy Corin being drenched
In seas of woe, to thee his plaints incline,
And at thy feet with tears doth sue for grace,
Which art the goddess of his chaste desire;
Let not thy frowns these labours poor deface
Although aloft they at the first aspire;
    And time shall come as yet unknown to men
    When I more large thy praises forth shall pen!

BARTHOLOMEW GRIFFIN

(d. 1602)

from *Fidessa*

II

How can that piercing crystal-painted eye,
    That gave the onset to my high aspiring.
Yielding each look of mine a sweet reply,
    Adding new courage to my heart's desiring,
How can it shut itself within her ark,
    And keep herself and me both from the light,
Making us walk in all misguiding dark,
    Aye to remain in confines of the night?
How is it that so little room contains it,
    That guides the orient as the world the sun,
Which once obscured most bitterly complains it,
    Because it knows and rules whate'er is done?
The reason is that they may dread her sight,
Who doth both give and take away their light.

IX

My spotless love that never yet was tainted,
　　My loyal heart that never can be moved,
My growing hope that never yet hath fainted,
　　My constancy that you full well have proved,
All these consented have to plead for grace
　　These all lie crying at the door of beauty; –
This wails, this sends out tears, this cries apace,
　　All do reward expect of faith and duty;
Now either thou must prove th' unkindest one,
　　And as thou fairest art must cruelest be,
Or else with pity yield unto their moan,
　　Their moan that ever will importune thee.
Ah, thou must be unkind, and give denial,
And I, poor I, must stand unto my trial!

XVII

Sweet stroke, – so might I thrive as I must praise–
    But sweeter hand that gives so sweet a stroke!
The lute itself is sweetest when she plays.
    But what hear I? A string through fear is broke!
The lute doth shake as if it were afraid.
    O sure some goddess holds it in her hand,
A heavenly power that oft hath me dismayed,
    Yet such a power as doth in beauty stand!
Cease lute, my ceaseless suit will ne'er be heard!
    Ah, too hard-hearted she that will not hear it!
If I but think on joy, my joy is marred;
    My grief is great, yet ever must I bear it;
But love 'twixt us will prove a faithful page,
And she will love my sorrows to assuage.

XXXVII

Fair is my love that feeds among the lilies,
    The lilies growing in that pleasant garden
Where Cupid's mount, that well beloved hill is,
    And where that little god himself is warden.
See where my love sits in the beds of spices,
    Beset all round with camphor, myrrh, and
                      roses,
And interlaced with curious devices,
    Which her from all the world apart incloses.
There doth she tune her lute for her delight,
    And with sweet music makes the ground to
                      move;
Whilst I, poor I, do sit in heavy plight,
    Wailing alone my unrespected love,
Not daring rush into so rare a place,
That gives to her, and she to it, a grace.

ANONYMOUS
(published 1597)

"Come away, come, sweet love"

COME AWAY, come, sweet love,
The golden morning breaks,
All the earth, all the air
Of love and pleasure speaks,
Teach thine arms then to embrace,
And sweet rosy lips to kiss,
And mix our souls in mutual bliss,
Eyes were made for beauty's grace,
Viewing, rueing love's long pain,
Procur'd by beauty's rude disdain.

Come away, come, sweet love,
The golden morning wastes,
While the sun from his sphere
His fiery arrows casts:
Making all the shadows fly,
Playing, staying in the grove,
To entertain the stealth of love,
Thither, sweet love, let us hie,

Flying, dying, in desire,
Wing'd with sweet hopes and heav'nly fire.

Come away, come, sweet love,
Do not in vain adorn
Beauty's grace that should rise
Like to the naked morn:
Lilies on the river's side,
And fair cyprian flowers new blown,
Desire no beauties but their own,
Ornament is nurse of pride,
Pleasure, measure, love's delight,
Haste then, sweet love, our wished flight.

ANONYMOUS

Madrigal

MY LOVE in her attire doth show her wit,
    It doth so well become her:
For every season she hath dressings fit,
    For winter, spring, and summer.
No beauty she doth miss,
    When all her robes are on:
But Beauty's self she is,
    When all her robes are gone.

ANONYMOUS

Aubade

STAY, O sweet, and do not rise!
   The light that shines comes from thine eyes;
The day breaks not: it is my heart,
   Because that you and I must part.
        Stay! or else my joys will die.
        And perish in their infancy.

ANTHONY MUNDAY
(1553-1633)

Beauty Bathing

BEAUTY SAT bathing by a spring
   Where fairest shades did hide her;
The winds blew calm, the birds did sing,
   The cool streams ran beside her.
My wanton thoughts enticed mine eye
   To see what was forbidden:
But better memory said, fie!
   So vain desire was chidden.
      Hey nonny, nonny, etc.

Into a slumber then I fell,
   When fond imagination
Seemed to see, but could not tell
   Her feature or her fashion.
But even as babes in dreams do smile,
   And sometime fall a-weeping,
So I awaked, as wise this while,
   As when I fell a-sleeping.
      Hey nonny, nonny, etc.

SIR PHILIP SIDNEY
(1554-1586)

from *The Countess of Pembroke's Arcadia*

"My true love hath my heart, and I have his"

MY TRUE love hath my heart, and I have his,
By just exchange one for the other given.
I hold his dear, and mine he cannot miss:
There never was a better bargain drive.
His heart in me keeps me and him inone;
My heart in him his thoughts and senses guides;
He loves my heart, for once it was his own;
I cherish his, because in me it bides,
His heart his wound received from my sight;
My heart was wounded with his wounded heart;
For as from me on him his hurt did light,
So still, methought, in me is hurt did light,
   Both equal hurt, in this change sought our
                    bliss:
   My true love hath my heart, and I have his.

"O my thought's sweet food, my, my only owner"

O MY thought's sweet food, my, my only owner,
  O my heavens for taste by heavenly pleasure,
Of the fair nymph born to do women honour,
                  Lady my Treasure.

Where be now those joys, that I lately tasted?
  Where be now those eyes ever inly persers?
Where be now those worlds never idly wasted,
                Wounds to rehearsers?

Where is ah that face, that a sun defaces?
  Where be those welcomes by no worth
                deserved?
Where be those movings, the delights, the
                graces?
                How be we swerved?

O hideous absence, by thee am I thralled.
  O my vain word gone, ruin of my glory.
O due allegiance, by thee am I called
                Still to be sorry.

But no more words, though words be spoken,
  Nor no more wording with a word to spill me.
Peace, due allegiance, duty must be broken,

If duty kill me.

Then come, O come, then I do come, receive me,
　Slay me not, for stay do not hide thy blisses,
But between those arms, never else do leave me;
　　　　Give me thy kisses.

O my thoughts' sweet food, my, my only owner,
　O my heavens for taste, by thy heavenly
　　　　　　pleasure,
O the fair nymph born to do women honour,
　　　　Lady my Treasure.

from *Sonnets of Astrophel and Stella*

6

SOME LOVERS speak when they their Muses
                     entertain,
Of hopes begot by fear, of wot not what desires;
Of force of heaven'ly beames, infusing hellish
                     pain;
  Of living deaths, deare wounds, faire storms
                 and freezing fires:
  Some one his song in *Jove*, and *Jove's* strange
                 tales attires,?
Bordered with bulls and swans, powdered with
                 golden raine:
Another humbler wit to shepheard's pipe retires
Yet hiding royal blood full oft in rural vaine.
  To some a sweetest plaint a sweetest stile
                 affords,
  While tears power out his ink, and sighs
                 breathe out his words:
His paper, pale dispair, and pain his pen doth
                 move.
  I can speak what I feel, and feel as much as
                 they,
  But think that all the Map of my state I

display,
When trembling voice brings forth that I do
Stella love.

STELLA, THE only planet of my light,
   Light of my life, and life of my desire,
Chief good whereto my hope doth only aspire,
World of my wealth, and heaven of my delight,
Why dost thou spend the treasures of thy spright,
   With voice more fit to wed Amphion's lyre,
   Seeking to quench in me the noble fire
Fed by thy worth, and kindled by thy sight?
And all in vain; for while thy breath most sweet
   With choicest words, thy words with reasons
                  rare,
Thy reasons firmly set on Virtue's feet,
   Labour to kill in me this killing care,
     O think I then, what paradise of joy
     It is, so fair a virtue to enjoy!

O JOY, too high for my low stile to show:
   O blisse, fit for a nobler state then me:
   Envie, put out thine eyes least thou do see
What Oceans of delight in me do flow.
My friend, that oft saw through all maskes my
                       woe,
   Come, come, and let me power my selfe on
                       thee;
   Gone is the winter of my miserie,
My spring appears; O see what here doth grow.
   For *Stella* hath with words where faith doth
                       shine,
Of her high heart giv'n me the monarchie:
I, I, O I may say that she is mine.
And though she give but thus conditionly?
   This realme of blisse, while vertuous course I
                       take,
   No king be crown'd, but they some convenant
                       make.

O KISSE, which doest those ruddie gemmes
                    impart,
Or gemmes, or fruits of new-found *Paradise*,
Breathing all blisse and sweetening to the heart,
    Teaching dumb lips a nobler exercise:
    O kisse, which soules, even soules together tie
By linke of *Love*, only Nature's art;
How faine would I paint thee to all men's eyes,
Or of thy gift at least shade out some part.
    But she forbids; with blushing words, she says
    She builds her fame on higher seated praise:
But my heart burnes, I cannot silent be.
    Then since (deare life) you faine would have
                    me peace,
    And I, mad with delight, want wit to cease,
Stop you my mouth with still kissing me.

NICHOLAS BRETON
(*c*. 1555-1626)

A Report Song

SHALL WE go dance the hay, the hay?
Never pipe could ever play
Better shepherd's roundelay.

Shall we go sing the song, the song?
Never Love did ever wrong.
Fair maids, hold hands all along.

Shall we go learn to woo, to woo?
Never thought came ever to,
Better deed could better do.

Shall we go learn to kiss, to kiss?
Never heart could ever miss
Comfort, where true meaning is.

Thus at base they run, they run,
When the sport was scarce begun.
But I waked, and all was done.

Oh That My Heart

OH THAT my heart could hit upon a strain
Would strike the music of my soul's desire;
Or that my soul could find that sacred vein
That sets the consort of the angels' choir.
Or that that spirit of especial grace
That cannot stoop beneath the state of heaven
Within my soul would take his settled place
With angels' *Ens*, to make his glory even.
Then should the name of my most gracious King,
And glorious God, in higher tunes be sounded
Of heavenly praise, than earth hath power to sing,
Where heaven, and earth, and angels, are
                              confounded.
  And souls may sing while all heart strings
      are broken;
  His praise is more than can in praise be
      spoken.

THOMAS LODGE
(1558-1625)

He Wrote This With a Pointed Diamond In Her
Glass

Think what I suffered, wanton, through thy
                 wildness,
When, traitor to my faith, thy looseness led thee;
Think how my mody wrath was turned to
                 mildness,
When I bad best, yet baser grooms did bed thee.
Think that the stain of beauty then is stainèd,
When lewd desires do alienate the heart;
Think that the love which will not be containèd
At last will grow to hate in spite of art.
Think that those wanton looks will have their
                 wrinkles,
And but by faith old age can merit nothing;
When time thy pale with purple over-sprinkles,
Faith is thy best, thy beauty is a woe-thing.
      In youth be true, and then in age resolve
                 thee,
      Friends will be friends, till time with them
                 dissolve thee.

from *Phillis*

IX

   The dewy roseate Morn had with her hairs
In sundry sorts the Indian clime adorned;
And now her eyes apparrelèd in tears,
The loss of lovely Memnon long had mourned,
   When as she spied the nymph whom I admire,
Combing her locks, of which the yellow gold
Made blush the beauties of her curlèd wire,
Which heaven itself with wonder might behold;
   Then red with shame, her reverend locks she
                       rent,
And weeping hid the beauty of her face,
The flower of fancy wrought such discontent;
The sighs which midst the air she breathed a
                    space,
   A three-days' stormy tempest did maintain,
   Her shame a fire, her eyes a swelling rain.

XIII

Love guides the roses of thy lips,
And flies about them like a bee;
If I approach he forward skips,
And if I kiss he stingeth me.
  Love in thine eyes doth build his bower,
And sleeps within their pretty shine;
And if I look the boy will lower,
And from their orbs shoots shafts divine.
  Love works thy heart within his fire,
And in my tears doth firm the same;
And if I tempt it will retire,
And of my plaints doth make a game.
  Love, let me cull her choicest flowers,
And pity me, and calm her eye,
Make soft her heart, dissolve her lowers,
Then will I praise thy deity.
  But if thou do not love, I'll truly serve her
  In spite of thee, and by firm faith deserve her.

XXXIV

I WOULD in rich and golden coloured raine,
With tempting showers in pleasant sort descend,
Into faire Phillis' lappe (my lovely friend)
When sleep her sense with slumber doth
                    restraine.
  I would be changed to a milk-white Bull,
When midst the gladsome fields she should
                    appeare,
By pleasant fineness to surprise my deere,
Whilest from their stalk, she pleasant flower did
                    pull:
  I were content to wearie out my paine,
To be Narsissus so she were a spring
To drowne in her those woes my heart do wring:
And more I wish transformed to remaine;
    That whilest I thus in pleasure's lappe did lie,
    I might refresh desire, which else would die.

RICHARD BARNFIELD
(1574-1627)

Sonnet

SWEET CORALL lips, where Nature's treasure
                lies,
    The balme of blisse, the soveraigne salve of
                sorow,
    The secret touch of love's heart-burning
                arrow,
Come quench my thirst oe else poor *Daphnis*
                dies.
One night I dream'd (alas twas but a Dreame)
    That I did feele the sweetness of the same,
    Where-with inspir'd, I young againe became,
And from my heart a spring of blood did streame,
But when I wak't, I found it nothing so,
    Save that my limbs (me thought) did waxe
                more strong
    And I more lusty far, and far more young.
This gift on him rich Nature did bestow.
    Then if in dreaming so, I so did speede,
    What should I doe, if I did so indeed?

WILLIAM PERCY
(1575-1648)

It Shall Be Said I Died For Coelia!

It shall be said I died for Coelia!
Then quick, thou grisly man of Erebus,
Transport me hence unto Proserpina,
To be adjudged as 'wilful amorous':
To be hung up within the liquid air,
For all the sighs which I in vain have wasted:
To be through Lethe's waters cleansèd fair,
For those dark clouds which have my looks
                    o'ercasted:
To be condemned to everlasting fire,
Because at Cupid's fire I wilful brent me;
And to be clad, for deadly dumps, in more.
    One solace I shall find, when I am over:
    It will be known I died a constant lover!

GILES FLETCHER
(1588?-1623)

from *Licia*

V

Love with her hair my love by force hath tied,
To serve her lips, her eyes, her voice, her hand;
I smiled for joy, when I the boy espied
To lie unchained and live at her command.
She if she look, or kiss, or sing, or smile,
Cupid withal doth smile, doth sing, doth kiss,
Lips, hands, voice, eyes, all hearts that may
                          beguile,
Because she scorns all hearts but only this.
Venus for this in pride began to frown
That Cupid, born a god, enthralled should be.
She in disdain her pretty son threw down,
And in his place, with love she chainèd me.
    So now, sweet love, though I myself be thrall,
    Not her a goddess, but thyself I call.

XIV

My love lay sleeping, where birds music made,
Shutting her eyes, disdainful of the light;
The heat was great but greater was the shade
Which her defended from his burning sight.
This Cupid saw, and came a kiss to take,
Sucking sweet nectar from her sugared breath;
She felt the touch, and blushed, and did awake,
Seeing t'was love, which she did think was death,
She cut his wings and causèd him to stay,
Making a vow, he should not thence depart,
Unless to her the wanton boy could pay
The truest, kindest and most loving heart.
    His feathers still she usèd for a fan,
    Till by exchange my heart his feathers won.

XXVI

I LIVE (sweete love) whereas the gentle winde
Murmures with sport, in midst of thickest bowes,
Where loving Wood-bine doth the Harbour
                      binde,
And chirping bird do echo forth my vowes;
Where strongest elm can scarce support the vine,
And sweetest flowres enameld have the ground,
Where Muses dwell: and yet heart repine
That on the earth so rare a place was found.
But winde delight: I wish to be content.
I praise the Wood-bine, but I take no joye:
I moane the birdes that musicke thus have spent:
As for the rest, they breede but mine annoye.
   Live thou (fayre Licia) in this place alone:
   Then shall I joye, though all of these were
                      gone.

GEORGE CHAPMAN
(1559?-1634)

Epithalamion Teratos, from *Hero and Leander*

COME, COME, dear Night, Love's mart of kisses,
Sweet close of his ambitious line,
The fruitful summer of his blisses,
Love's glory doth in darkness shine.
O come, soft rest of cares, come Night,
Come naked Virtue's only tire,
The reaped harvest of the light,.
Bound up in sheaves of sacred fire.
   Love calls to war,
   Sighs his alarms,
   Lips his swords are,
   The field his arms.
Come, Night, and lay thy velvet hand
On glorious Day's outfacing face,
And all thy crowned flames command
For torches to our nuptial grace.
   Love calls to war,
   Sighs his alarms,
   Lips his swords are,

 The field his arms.
No need have we of factious Day,
To cast in envy of thy peace
Her balls of discord in thy way:
Here Beauty's day doth never cease;
Day is abstracted here,
And varied in a triple sphere.
Hero, Alcame, Mya outshine thee,
Ere thou come here let Thetis thrice refine thee.

 Love calls to war,
 Sighs his alarms,
 Lips his swords are,
 The field his arms.
The evening star I see:
Rise, youths, the evening star
Helps Love to summon war;
Both now embracing be.
Rise, youths, Love's rite claims more than
       banquets, rise.
Now the bright marigolds that deck the skies,
Phoebus' celestial flowers, that (contrary
To his flowers here) ope when he shuts his eye,
And shut when he doth open, crown your sports.
Now Love in Night, and Night in love exhorts
Courtship and dances. All your parts employ,
And suit Night's rich expansure with your joy.
Love paints his longings in sweet virgins' eyes:
Rise, youths, Love's right claims more than

      banquets, rise.
Rise, virgins, let fair nuptial loves enfold
Your fruitless breasts: the maidenheads ye hold
Are not your own alone, but parted are;
Part in disposing them your parents share,
And that a third part is; so must ye save
Your loves a third, and you your thirds must
       have.
Love paints his longings in sweet virgins' eyes:
Rise, youths, Love's rite claims more than
      banquets, rise.

SAMUEL DANIEL
(1562-1619)

from *Sonnets to Delia*

6

FAIR IS my Love, and cruel as she's fair;
    Her brow shades frowns, although her eyes are
                sunny;
Her smiles are lightning, though her pride
                despair;
    And her disdains are gall, her favours honey.
A modest maid, deckt with a blush of honour,
    Whose feet to tread green paths of youth and
                love,
The wonder of all eyes that look upon her,
    Sacred on earth, designed a saint above!
Chastity and Beauty, which were deadly foes,
    Live reconciled friends within her brow;
And had the Pity to conjoin with those,
    Then who had heard the plaints I utter now?
      For had she not been fair, and thus unkind,

My Muse had slept, and none had known my mind.

12

My spotless love hovers with purest wings
    About the temple of the proudest frame,
    Where blaze those lights, fayres of earthly
                things,
    Which clear our clouded world with
                brightest flame.
M' ambitious thoughts, confined in her face,
    Affect no honour but what she can give:
    My hopes do rest in limits of her grace;
    I weigh no comfort unless she relieve.
For she that can my heart imparadize,
    Holds in her fairest hand what dearest is:
    My fortune's wheel's the circle of her eyes,
    Whose rowling grace deign once a turn of
                bliss.
All my live's sweet consists in her alone,
So much I love the most unloving one.

35

BUT LOVE whilst that thou mayst be loved again,
   Now whilst thy May hath filled thy lap with
             flowers,
Now whilst thy beauty bears without a stain;
   Now use thy summer miles ere winter lours.
And whilst thou spread'st unto the rising sun
   The fairest flower that ever saw the light,
Now joy thy time before thy sweet be done:
   And, Delia, think thy morning must have
             night,
And what thy brightness sets at length to west,
   When thou wilt close up that which now
             thou showest;
And think the same becomes thy fading best,
   Which then shall hide it most and cover
             lowest.
      Men do not weigh the stalk for that it
             was,
      When once they find her flower, her
             glory, pass.

READE IN my face a volume of dispayres,
   The wayling Iliads of my tragicke woe,
   Drawne with my blood, and printed with my
                cares,
   Wrought by her hand that I have honoured so:
Who whilst I burne, she sings at my soule's
                wrack,
   Looking aloft from Turret of her pride:
   There my soule's Tyrant joyes her, in the sack
   Of her owne seate, whereof I made her guide.
There do these smokes that from affliction rise
   Serve as an incense to a cruel Dame;
   A Sacrifice thrice-gratefull to her eyes,
   Because their powre serve to exact the same.
Thus ruines she (to satisfie her will)
The Temple, where her name was honour'd still.

47

BEAUTY, SWEET Love, is like the morning dew,
    Whose short refresh upon the tender green
Cheers for a time, but till the sun doth shew,
    And straight 'tis gone as it had never been.
Soon doth it fade that makes the fairest flourish
    Short is the glory of the blushing rose,
The hue which thou so carefully dost nourish,
    Yet which at length thou must be forced to
                        lose.
When thou, surcharged with burden of thy years,
    Shalt bend thy wrinkles homeward to the
                        earth,
And that in beauty's lease expired appears
    The date of age, the calends of our death –
        But ah! no mor; this must not be
                        foretold,
        For women grieve to think they must be
                        old.

HENRY CONSTABLE
(1562-1613)

from *Sonnets to Diana*

Upon Occasion of Her Walking In a Garden (1.9)

MY LADY'S presence makes the roses red,
Because to see her lips they blush with shame.
The lily's leaves for envy pale became,
And her white hands in them this envy bred.
The marigold the leaves abroad doth spread,
Because the sun's and her power is the same.
The violet of purple colour came,
Dyed in the blood she made my heart to shed.
In brief, all flowers from her their virtue take;
From her sweet breath their sweet smells do
                              proceed;
The living heat which her eyebeams doth make
Warmeth the ground and quickeneth the seed.
The rain wherewith she watereth the flowers,
Falls from mine eyes which she dissolves in
                              showers.

To His Lady's Hand Upon Occasion of Her Glove
Which In Her Absence He Kissed (2.9)

SWEET HAND, the sweet but cruel bow thou art,
From whence at me five ivory arrows fly;
So with five wounds at once I wounded lie,
Bearing my breast the print of every dart.
Saint Francis had the like, yet felt no smart,
Where I in living torments never die.
His wounds were in his hands and feet; where I
All these five helpless wounds feel in my heart.
Now, as Saint Francis, if a saint am I,
The bow that shot these shafts a relic is;
I mean the hand, which is the reason why
So many for devotion thee would kiss:
And some thy glove kiss as a thing divine,
This arrows' quiver, and this relic's shrine.

Of the End and Death of His Love (4.6)

EACH DAY, new proofs of new despair I find,
That is, new deaths. No marvel then, though I
Make exile my last help; to th'end mine eye
Should not behold the death to me assigned.
Not that from death absence might save my mind,
But that it might take death more patiently;
Like him, the which by judge condemned to die,
To suffer with more ease, his eyes doth blind.
Your lips in scarlet clad, my judges be,
Pronouncing sentence of eternal 'No!'
Despair, the hangman that tormenteth me;
The death I suffer is the life I have.
For only life doth make me die in woe,
And only death I for my pardon crave.

"To live in hell, and heaven to behold" (6.2)

TO LIVE in hell, and heaven to behold;
   To welcome life, and die a living death;
To sweat with heat, and yet be freezing cold;
   To grasp at stars, and lie the earth beneath;
To tread a maze that never shall have end;
   To burn in sighs, and starve in daily tears;
To climb a hill, and never to descend;
   Giants to kill, and quake at childish fears;
To pine for food, and watch th' Hesperides tree;
   To thirst for drink, and nectar still to draw;
To live accursed, women, hold blest to be,
   And weep those wrongs which never creature
              saw:
    If this be love, if love in these be founded,
    My heart is love, for these in it are grounded.

"Love hath I followed all too long, nought gaining" (6.9)

LOVE HATH I followed all too long, nought
                              gaining;
And sighed I have in vain to sweet what smarteth,
But from his brow a fiery arrow parteth,
Thinking that I should him resist not plaining.
But cowardly my heart submiss remaining,
Yields to receive what shaft thy fair eye darteth.
Well do I see thine eye my bale imparteth,
And that save death no hope I am detaining.
For what is he can alter fortune's sliding?
One in his bed consumes his life away,
Other in wars, another in the sea;
The like effects in me have their abiding;
For heavens avowed my fortune should be such,
That I should die by loving far too much.

"My God, my God, how much I love my goddess"
(6.10)

MY GOD, my God, how much I love my goddess,
Whose virtues rare, unto the heavens arise!
My God, my God, how much I love her eyes
One shining bright, the other full of hardness!
My God, my God, how much I love her wisdom,
Whose works may ravish heaven's richest maker!
Of whose eyes' joys if I might be partaker
Then to my soul a holy rest would come.
My God, how much I love to hear her speak!
Whose hands I kiss and ravished oft rekisseth,
When she stands wotless whom so much she
                        blesseth.
Say then, what mind this honest love would
                        break;
Since her perfections pure, withouten blot,
Makes her beloved of thee, she knoweth not?

MICHAEL DRAYTON
(1563-1631)

from *Idea*

4

BRIGHT STAR of beauty, on whose eyelids sit
A thousand nymph-like and enamoured graces,
The goddesses of memory and wit,
Which there in order take their several places;
In whose dear bosom, sweet delicious love
Lays down his quiver which he once did bear,
Since he that blessèd paradise did prove,
And leaves his mother's lap to sport him there
Let others strive to entertain with words
My soul is of a braver mettle made;
I hold that vile which vulgar wit affords;
In me's that faith which time cannot invade.
   Let what I praise be still made good by you;
   Be you most worthy whilst I am most true!

AN EVIL spirit, your beauty, haunts me still,
　　Wherewith (alas) I have been long possessed,
Which ceaseth not to tempt me to each ill,
　　Nor gives me once but one poor minute's rest.
In me it speaks, whether I sleep or wake,
　　And when by means to drive it out I try,
With greater torments then it me doth take,
　　And tortures me in most extremity.
Before my face it lays down my despairs,
　　And hastes me on unto a sudden death,
Now tempting me to drown myself in tears,
　　And then in sighing to give up my breath.
　　　　Thus am I still provoked to every evil
　　　　By this good wicked spirit, sweet angel
　　　　　　　　　　devil.

41

Love's Lunacie

WHY DO I speake of Joy, or write of Love,
When my heart is the very Den of Horror,
And in my Soule the paines of hell I prove,
With all his Torments and Infernal terror?
What should I say? What yet remaines to do?
My Brain is dry with weeping all too long;
My Sighs be spent in utt'ring of my Woe,
And I want words wherewith to tell my Wrong:
But still distracted in Love's Lunacie,
And Bedlam-like, thus raving in my Griefe,
Now rail upon Her Haire, then on her Eye;
Now call her Goddesse, then I call her Thiefe;
    Now I deny Her, then I do confess Her,
    Now do I curse Her, then again I blesse Her.

61

SINCE THERE'S no help, come let us kiss and
part,
Nay, I have done: you get no more of me,
And I am glad, yea, glad with all my heart,
That thus so cleanly I myself can free,
Shake hands for ever, cancel all our vows,
And when we meet at any time again,
Be it not seen in either of our brows,
That we one jot of former love retain;
Now at the last gasp, of love's latest breath,
When, his pulse failing, passion speechless lies,
When faith is kneeling by his bed of death,
And innocence is closing up his eyes,
Now if thou would'st, when all have given him
over,
From death to life, thou might'st him yet
recover.

"So well I love thee, as without thee I"

SO WELL I love thee, as without thee I
Love nothing; if I might choose, I'd rather die
Than be one day debarr'd thy company.

Since beasts, and plants do grow, and live and
                                    move,
Beasts are those men, that such a life approve:
He only lives, that deadly is in love.

The corn that in the ground is sown first dies
And of one seed do many ears arise:
Love, this world's corn, by dying multiplies.

The seeds of love first by thy eyes were thrown
Into a ground untill'd, a heart unknown
To bear such fruit, till by thy hands 'twas sown.

Look as your looking-glass by chance may fall,
Divide and break in many pieces small
And yet shows forth the selfsame face in all:

Proportions, features, graces just the same,
And in the smallest piece as well the name
Of fairest one deserves, as in the richest frame.

So all my thoughts are pieces but of you
Which put together makes a glass so true
As I therein no other's face but yours can view.

CHRISTOPHER MARLOWE
(1564-1593)

The Passionate Sheepheard to His Love

COME LIVE with me, and be my love,
And we will all the pleasure prove,
That Valleys, groves, hills and fields,
Woods, or steepy mountain yields.

And we will sit upon the Rocks,
Seeing the Shepherds feed their flocks,
By shallow Rivers, to whose falls,
Melodious birds sing Madrigalls.

And I will make thee beds of Roses,
And a thousand fragrant poesies,
A cap of flowers, and a kirtle,
Embroidered all with leaves of Myrtle.

A gown made of the finest wool,
Which from our pretty Lambs we pull,
Fair lined slippers for the cold:
With buckles of the purest gold.

A belt of straw, and Ivy buds,
With Coral clasps and Amber studs,
And if these pleasures may thee move,
Come live with me, and be my love.

The Shepherds Swains shall dance and sing,
For thy delight each May morning,
If these delights thy mind may move;
Then live with me, and be my love.

WILLIAM SHAKESPEARE
(1564-1616)

from *The Sonnets*

18

SHALL I compare thee to a summer's day?
Thou art more lovely and more temperate:
Rough winds do shake the darling buds of May,
And summer's lease hath all too short a date:
Sometimes too hot the eye of heaven shines,
And often is his gold complexion dimm'd,
And every fair from fair sometime declines,
By chance or nature's changing course
                              untrimm'd:
But thy eternal summer shall not fade
Nor lose possession of that fair thou ow'st,
Nor shall Death brag thou wander'st in his shade,
When in eternal lines to time thou grow'st:
    So long as men can breathe or eyes can see,
    So long lives this, and this gives life to thee.

20

A WOMAN'S face with nature's own hand painted
Hast thou, the master-mistress of my passion;
A woman's gentle heart, but not acquainted
With shifting change as is false women's
                      fashion;
An eye more bright than theirs, less false in
                      rolling,
Gilding the object whereupon it gazeth;
A man in hue all hues in so controlling,
Which steals men's eyes and women's souls
                      amazeth:
And for a woman wert thou first created, –
Till nature as she wrought thee fell a-doting,
And by addition me of thee defeated,
By adding one thing to my purpose nothing.
    But since she prick'd thee out for women's
                      pleasure,
    Mine be thy love and thy love's use their
                      pleasure.

TAKE ALL my loves, my love, yea, take them all:
What hast thou then more than thou hadst
before?
No love, my love, that thou mayst true love call –
All mine was thine, before thou hadst this more.
Then if for my love thou my love receivest,
I cannot blame thee, for my love thou usest, –
But yet be blam'd, if thou this self deceivest
By wilful taste of what thy self refusest.
I do forgive thy robbery, gentle thief,
Although thou steal thee all my poverty:
And yet love knows it is a greater grief
To bear love's wrong than hate's knowing injury.
> Lascivious grave, in whom all ill well shows,
> Kill me with spites, yet we must not be foes.

SWEET LOVE, renew thy force; be it not said
Thy edge should blunter be than appetite,
Which but today by feeding is allay'd,
Tomorrow sharpen'd in his former might:
So, love, be thou; although today thou fill
Thy hungry eyes even till they wink with fulness,
Tomorrow see again, and do not kill
The spirit of love with a perpetual dulness:
Let this sad interim like the ocean be
Which parts the shore where two contracted new
Come daily to the banks, that when they see
Return of love more blest may be the view:
    As call it winter, which being full of care
    Makes summer's welcome, thrice more
                        wish'd, more rare.

TO ME, fair friend, you can never be old,
For as you were when first your eye I eyed
Such seems your beauty still: three winters cold
Have from the forests shook three summer's
                                    pride,
Three beauteous springs to yellow autumn turn'd
In process of the seasons have I seen,
Three April perfumes in three hot Junes burn'd,
Since first I saw you fresh which yet are green.
Ah yet doth beauty like a dial hand
Steal from his figure and no pace perceiv'd,
So your sweet hue, which methinks still doth
                                    stand,
Hath motion, and mine eye may be deceiv'd,
    For fear of which hear this, thou age unbred:
    Ere you were born was beauty's summer
                                    dead.

LET ME not to the marriage of true minds
Admit impediments: love is not love
Which alters when it alteration finds,
Or bends with the remover to remove.
Oh no! it is an ever-fixed mark
That looks on tempests and is never shaken;
It is the star to every wandering bark,
Whose worth's unknown although his height be
                      taken.
Love's not Time's fool, though rosy lips and
                      cheeks
Within his bending sickle's compass come;
Love alters not with his brief hours and weeks,
But bears it out even to the edge of doom.
    If this be error and upon me prov'd,
    I never writ, nor no man ever lov'd.

129

THE EXPENSE of spirit in a waste of shame
Is lust in action; and till action, lust
Is perjur'd, murderous, bloody, full of blame,
Savage, extreme, rude, cruel, not to trust;
Enjoy'd no sooner but despised straight;
Past reason hunted; and no sooner had,
Past reason hated, as a swallow'd bait
On purpose laid to make the taker mad, –
Mad in pursuit, and in possession so;
Had, having, and in quest to have, extreme;
A bliss in proof; and prov'd, a very woe;
Before, a joy propos'd; behind, a dream.
    All this the world well knows; yet none
                    knows well
    To shun the heaven that leads men to this
                    hell.

MY LOVE is as a fever, longing still
For that which longer nurseth the disease,
Feeding on that which doth preserve the ill,
The uncertain sickly appetite to please.
My reason, the physician to my love,
Angry that his prescriptions are not kept,
Hath left me, and I desperate now approve
Desire is death, which physic did except.
Past cure I am now reason is past care,
And frantic mad with evermore unrest;
My thoughts and my discourse as madmen's are,
At random from the truth, vainly express'd:
    For I have sworn thee fair, and thought thee
                    bright,
    Who art black as hell, as dark as night.

from *Venus and Adonis*

*"This said, impatience chokes her pleading
tongue"*

THIS SAID, impatience chokes her pleading
tongue,
And swelling passion doth provoke a pause;
Red cheeks and fiery eyes blaze forth he wrong;
Being judge in love, she cannot right her cause:
And now she weeps, and now she fain would
speak,
And now her sobs do her intendments break.

Sometimes she shakes her head and then his
hand,
Now gazeth she on him, now on the ground;
Sometimes her arms infold him like a band:
She would, he will not in her arms be bound;
And when from thence he struggles to be
gone,
She locks her lily fingers one in one.

'Fondling,' she saith, 'since I have hemm'd thee
here
Within the circuit of this ivory pale,

I'll be a park, and thou shalt be my deer;
Feed where thou wilt, on mountain or in dale:
 Graze on my lips; and if those hills be dry,
 Stray lower, where the pleasant fountains lie.

Within this limit is relief enough,
Sweet bottom-grass and high delightful plain,
Round rising hillocks, brakes obscure and rough,
To shelter thee from tempest and from rain
 Then be my deer, since I am such a park;
 No dog shall rouse thee, though a thousand
      bark.'

At this Adonis smiles as in disdain,
That in each cheek appears a pretty dimple:
Love made those hollows, if himself were slain,
He might be buried in a tomb so simple;
 Foreknowing well, if there he came to lie,
 Why, there Love lived and there he could not
      die.

These lovely caves, these round enchanting pits,
Open'd their mouths to swallow Venus' liking.
Being mad before, how doth she now for wits?
Struck dead at first, what needs a second striking?
 Poor queen of love, in thine own law forlorn,
 To love a cheek that smiles at thee in scorn!

"But love, first learned in a lady's eyes"

BUT LOVE, first learned in a lady's eyes,
Lives not alone immured in the brain,
But with the motion of all elements
Courses as swift as thought in every power,
And gives to every power a double power,
Above their functions and their offices.
It adds a precious seeing to the eye:
A lover's eyes will gaze an eagle blind.
A lover's ear will hear the lowest sound,
When the suspicious head of theft is stopp'd.
Love's feeling is more soft and sensible
Than are the tender horns of cockled snails;
Love's tongue proves dainty Bacchus gross in
taste.
For valour, is not Love a Hercules,
Still climbing trees in the Hesperides?
Subtle as Sphinx; as sweet and musical
As bright Apollo's lute, strung with his hair.
And when Love speaks, the voice of all the gods
Make heaven drowsy with the harmony.
Never durst poet touch a pen to write
Until his ink were temp'red with love's sighs;
O, then his lines would ravish savage ears,
And plant in tyrants mild humility.
From women's eyes this doctrine I derive.

❀ | | |

They sparkle still the right Promethean fire;
They are the books, the arts, the academes,
That show, contain, and nourish, all the world,
Else none at all in aught proves excellent.

(Berowne *in Love's Labour's Lost,* 4.3.323-350)

"Gallop apace, you fiery-footed steeds"

GALLOP APACE, you fiery-footed steeds
Towards Phoebus' lodging; such a waggoner
As Phaethon would whip you to the west,
And bring in cloudy night immediately.
Spread thy close curtain, love-performing night,
That runaways' eyes may wink, and Romeo
Leap to these arms, untalk'd of and unseen.
Lovers can see to do their amorous rites
By their own beauties; or if love be blind,
It best agrees with night. Come, civil night,
Thou sober-suited matron, all in black,
And learn me how to lose a winning match,
Play'd for a pair of stainless maidenhoods;
Hood my unmann'd blood, bating in my cheeks,
With thy black mantle, till strange love, grown
                                    bold,
Think true love acted simple modesty.
Come, night; come, Romeo; come, thou day in
                                    night;
For thou wilt lie upon the wings of night
Whiter than new snow on a raven's back.
Come, gentle night, come, loving black-brow'd
                                    night,
Give me my Romeo; and, when he shall die,

Take him and cut him out in little stars,
And he will make the face of heaven so fine
That all the world will be in love with night,
And pay no worship to the garish sun.

(Juliet in *Romeo and Juliet*, 3.1.1-25)

THOMAS CAMPION
(1567-1620)

"My sweetest Lesbia, let us live and love"

MY SWEETEST Lesbia, let us live and love;
And, though the sager sort our deeds reprove,
Let us not weigh them. Heaven's great lamps do
                              dive
Into their west, and straight again revive.
But soon as once set is our little light,
Then must we sleep one ever-during night.

If all would lead their lives in love like me,
Then bloody swords and armour should not be;
No drum, no trumpet peaceful sleeps should
                              move,
Unless alarm came from the camp of Love.
But fools do live and waste their little light,
And seek with pain their ever-during night.

When timely death my life and fortune ends,
Let not my hearse be vexed with mourning

friends,
But let all lovers, rich in triumph, come
And with sweet pastimes grace my happy tomb.
And, Lesbia, close up thou my little light,
And crown with love my ever-during night.

"What then is love but mourning?"

WHAT THEN is love but mourning?
  What desire, but a self-burning?
Till she that hates doth love return,
Thus will I mourn, thus will I sing,
  Come away, come away, my darling.

Beauty is but a blooming,
  Youth in his glory entombing;
Time hath a wheel, which none can stay:
Then come away, while thus I sing,
  Come away, come away, my darling.

Summer in winter fadeth;
  Gloomy night heav'nly light shadeth:
Like to the morn are Venus flowers;
Such are her howers: then will I sing,
  Come away, come away, my darling.

"Hark, all you ladies that do weep"

HARK, ALL you ladies that do sleep,
    The fairy queen Prosperina
Bids you awake, and pity them that weep.
      You may do in the dark
        What the day doth forbid.
      Fear not the dogs that bark;
        Night will have all hid.

But if you let your lovers moan,
    The fairy queen Prosperina
Will send abroad her fairies every one,
      That shall pinch black and blue
        Your white hands and fair arms,
      That did not kindly rue
        Your paramours' harms.

In myrtle arbours on the downs,
    The fairy queen Prosperina,
This night by moonshine, leading merry rounds,
      Holds a watch with sweet love,
        Down the dale, up the hill;
      No complaints or groans may move
        Their holy vigil.

All you that will hold watch with Love,

The fairy queen Prosperina
Will make you fairer than Dione's dove.
Roses red, lilies white,
And the clear damask hue,
Shall on your cheeks alight.
Love will adorn you.

All you that love or loved before,
The fairy queen Prosperina
Bids you increase that loving humour more.
They that have not yet fed
On delight amorous,
She vows that they shall lead
Apes in Avernus.

Laura

ROSE-CHEEKED Laura, come;
Sing thouh smoothily with thy beauty's
Silent music, either other
    Sweetly gracing.

Lovely forms do flow
From concent divinely framèd;
Heaven is music, and thy beauty's
    Birth is heavenly.

These dull notes we sing
Discords need for helps to grace them;
Only beauty purely loving
    Knows no discord.

But still moves delight,
Like clear springs renewed by flowing,
Ever perfect, ever in them-
      selves eternal.

A Lover's Plea

SHALL I come, sweet Love, to thee,
    When the evening beams are set?
Shall I not excluded be?
    Will you find no feignèd let?
Let me not, for pity, more
Tell the long hours at your door.

Who can tell what thief or foe
    In the covert of the night
For his prey will work my woe,
    Or through wicked foul despite?
So may I die unredressed.
Ere my long love be possessed.

But to let such dangers pass,
    Which a lover's thoughts disdain,
'Tis enough in such a place
    To attend love's joys in vain.
Do not mock me in thy bed,
While these cold nights freeze me dead.

JOHN DONNE
(1572-1631)

from *Elegy: To His Mistress On Going to Bed*

LICENCE MY roving hands, and let them go
Before, behind, between, above, below.
O my America, my new found land,
My kingdom, safeliest when with one man
                              manned,
My mine of precious stones, my empery,
How blessed am I in this discovering thee!
To enter in these bonds, is to be free;
Then where my hand is set, my seal shall be.
Full nakedness, all joys are due to thee.
As souls unbodied, bodies unclothed must be,
To taste whole joys.

BEN JONSON
(1573-1637)

To Celia

COME MY Celia, let us prove,
While we may, the sports of love;
Time will not be ours, for ever:
He, at length, our good will sever.
Spend not then his gifts in vain.
Sunnes, that set, may rise again:
But if once we loose this light,
'Tis, with us, perpetual night.
Why should we defer our joys?
Fame, and rumour are but toys.
Cannot we delude the eyes
Of a few poor houshold spies?
Or his easier ears beguile,
So removed by our wile?
'Tis no sin, loves fruit to steale,
But the sweet theft to reveal:
To be taken, to be seen,
These have crimes accounted been.

A GALLERY OF POETS

Elizabeth I, anonymous artist, 1575,
National Portrait Gallery, London

Sir Walter Raleigh, by the 'H' Monogrammist, 1588

Edmund Spenser

Sir Philip Sidney, National Portrait Gallery, London

Samuel Daniel

Henry Constable

Michael Drayton

Anonymous, Christopher Marlowe (?), 1585

William Shakespeare

Thomas Campion, National Portrait Gallery, London

John Donne

A NOTE ON ELIZABETHAN LOVE POETRY

Still today Elizabeth I presides over the Eliza-
bethan age, as the greatest monarch Britain's ever
had, the goddess of the greatest epoch of British
poetry. Elizabeth I appropriated the cult of the
Virgin Mary, styling herself as the Virgin Queen
of an Empire, according to Frances Yates:

> The bejewelled and painted images of the
> Virgin Mary had been cast out of churches and
> monasteries, but another bejewelled and
> painted image was set up in court, and went in
> progress through the land for her worshippers
> to adore. The cult of the Virgin was regarded as
> one of the chief abuses of the unreformed

Church, but it would be, perhaps, extravagant to suggest that, in a Christian country, the worship of the state Virgo was deliberately intended to take its place.[1]

This changeover from Catholic to Anglican allegiance is nothing new: many other monarchs and leaders have appropriated some mass feeling or politics for their own purposes. The power and influence of Elizabeth I and her 'nearly fifty years of myth-making', as Steve Davies (1986) puts it, extended through the ages. It did not stop with her death; as Maureen Sabine explains how Elizabeth and her court rewrote Christianity, so the Queen of Heaven became the Queen of Britain:

> Immediately upon her coronation, she took steps to suppress the belief that the mass was an offering of the true body of Christ which had really issued from he body of the Virgin Mary. In subsuming not only Corpus Christi but the fears of Mary to the propaganda of her provident rule, she made it clear that it was no longer Christ and his Mother but her body which constituted the immutable and vernal life of the church. Her tenacious hold over English social life as reigning queen for nearly fifty years, her remarkable longevity and robustness of person and her immersion in the Marian role of ageless virgin-mother-spouse

consecrated to her people helped to sub-
stantiate this monumental lie.[2]

Edmund Spenser created a myth or drama of
England in his poetry. The 'dream' occurs
throughout his poetry, but finds its most
concentrated expression in *The Faerie Queene*,
with its epic treatment of the 'dream of Albion', a
myth-making vision of Britain as the expression
of Elizabeth I's magnificence, and vice versa. *The
Faerie Queene* is an astonishing work, by any
standards, and it dwarfs, at times, even those
other creation of the Renaissance that are so
revered by readers and critics – Marlowe's *Doctor
Faustus*, Shakespeare's plays and Sidney's
Astrophel and Stella.

Francesco Petrarch's influence, can be felt
throughout the history of English poetry, and
very much in Elizabethan love poetry. One finds
Petrarch most obviously in Thomas Wyatt,
Shakespeare, John Donne, and the Elizabethan
sonneteers: Samuel Daniel, Sir Philip Sidney,
Michael Drayton and Edmund Spenser. One could
write a volume or two on Petrarch's influence on
the Renaissance poets of Britain. One sees
Petrarch in those conceits and oppositions, for
instance, where Wyatt speaks of burning and

freezing with love. In his *Delia*, Samuel Daniel laments that he is not as great a poet as Petrarch: he loves just as much, even if he can't describe his fervour in the same fluid, luminous rhymes as the master Italian poet:

> Though thou, a Laura, hast no Petrarch found,
>   In base attire yet clearly beauty shines.
> And I, though born within a colder clime,
>   Do feel mine inward heat as great, I
>   know it;
> He never had more faith, although more rhyme;
> I love as well, though he could better show it.

Sir Philip Sidney noted the self-deceit and self-manufacture of love poetry, when he wrote in a sonnet in *Astrophel and Stella*:

> It is most true what we call Cupid's dart
> An image in which for ourselves we carve...

Love and love poetry is indeed something humans carve for themselves. After all, this heterosexual, bourgeois, romantic love is not for the stars, the grass, the animals, but only for humans. The Elizabethan or Renaissance love poem was as much artifice as emotion; perhaps the ratio was more like 10% love and 90% art. Few of the Elizabethan love poets, for instance, were actually in love with the people they were writing about in their polished verses, as Michael Spiller notes:

> Why should a number of sonneteers have written love-poetry to women with whom they were not in love? Or to quite nonexistent women? Why should Robert Sidney have written a Petrarchan sequence of passionate complaint and melancholy while very happily and romantically married to his wife, Barbara Gamage? And why are so many sonnets translations or adaptions of other writers' work? One or two writers did indeed write their sonnets to women with whom they were fully and feasibly in love – Edmund Spenser, for example, and Drummond of Hawthornden (probably)… (125)

Sidney, in a first line of a sonnet from *Astrophel and Stella*, described precisely the origin of love poetry in emotional loss and sexual lack: 'O absent presence *Stella* is not here…' (106) This is precisely where all the pain of love stems from, this Lacanian lack, which produces desire. The love poet is out of love, so s/he writes of love, wanting to be back in love. It's a simple equation, explaining also the emphasis in patriarchal poetry on love and death, on the connections between sex and pain. For, simply, to be out of love is to be not as alive as in love. So the out-of-love state is likened to death, the death-in-life, as some poets call it. The goal is not so much the beloved as love. For love poets are 'in love with love', to use St Bernard's terms, so apposite here. The love poem, then, arises from the lack, it fills the space between the lover and the loved. It becomes the æsthetic-ization of love, love refined and distilled. As Michael Spiller writes:

> Desire…is the sense of an absence, or, more, exactly, a need to abolish an absence. It was Petrarch's extraordinary achievement to find in the sonnet a space where the movement between the desiring /I/ and its goal could be rhetorically mapped, by various linguistic devices that became the currency of poetic Europe. Thereafter, however desire might specifically be focused, the sonnet could express it, and Petrarchan love becomes a master analogy for all desire… (125)

William Shakespeare's *Sonnets* are central to his art. They display Shakespeare's poetic talent at its height. The *Sonnets* are the great love poem sequence in British poetry, as well as being the longest single group of English Renaissance sonnets. They rival in grandeur, skill and cleverness the poetic sequence from which they ultimately derive (via Sir Thomas Wyatt): Petrarch's *Rime*. In Shakespeare, introspection and self-analysis is as rigorous as in Petrarch's *Canzoniere*, but Shakespeare's bitterness and sense of irony is more deeply ingrained than in Petrarch. Shakespeare's *Sonnets* came late in the development of the Petrarchan sonnet sequence. They are decadent, late efforts of an already (by the 1590s) old-fashioned poetic form. Yet Shakespeare manages to infuse the form with an extraordinary power and magic. The *Sonnets*, indeed, contain some of the most marvellous moments in any (English) poetry. The magnificence of the opening lines of the *Sonnets*, for instance, is undeniable:

> Shall I compare thee to a summer's day? (18.1)
> Full many a glorious morning have I seen
> Flatter the mountain tops with sovereign eye,
> Kissing with golden face the meadows green,
>
> Gilding pale streams with heavenly alchemy
> (33.1-4)
>
> Take all my loves, my love, yea, take them all
> (40.1)
>
> Sweet love, renew thy force (56.1)

Let me not to the marriage of true minds
Admit impediments: love is not love
Which alters when it alteration finds,
Or bends with the remover to remove. (116.1-4)

My love is as a fever, longing still (147.1)

Formally, Shakespeare used the ordinary
sonnet rhyme scheme of abab, cdcd, efef, gg, 4 + 4
+ 4 + 2, a pattern made popular by the Earl of
Surrey in Tottel's *Miscellany*. This Surrey sonnet
form, like Thomas Wyatt's model (abba, abba,
cddc, ee), was easier for English poets to use than
the Petrarchan form of abab, abab, cde, cde.
Shakespeare never employs the Italian sestet, the
octave abba, cddc, and never crossed the 'turn' of
the sonnet, between the octave and the sestet
(except in the list poem, and in sonnet 148). The
octave and the sestet were nearly always kept
distinct. Shakespeare kept a distinct statement in
each quatrain and the couplet. The couplet was
nearly always a separate syntactical unit. For all
his other innovations, in the *Sonnets* Shake-
speare is formally uninventive and conservative,
preferring to stick to Surrey's rhyme scheme.
Other writers surpassed him for inventiveness
(such as Donne, Herbert, Milton, Spenser and
Lock). Nearly all of the *Sonnets* are regular; only
two sonnets are irregular: 126 with its twelve

lines, and the fifteen line sonnet 99. Sonnet 145 is in tetrameters. There are few sonnets that are *not* addressed to the beloved; there are no dialogue sonnets, many puns and convoluted metaphors, but no word games such as acrostics, tails, anagrams or reversible lines. There are no dialogues with other poets, either British or European. None of Shakespeare's *Sonnets* has been translated or adapted from another source (as Wyatt had done so skillfully with Petrarch).

Yet, despite his formal conservatism, Shakespeare's *Sonnets* are without doubt the finest sonnet sequence in English, surpassing Spenser's *Amoretti*, Drayton's *Idea* or Sidney's *Astrophel and Stella*. The Bard's ability to create word magic remains undiminished, even after centuries of quotation and discussion. It is the same with the plays – most obviously *Hamlet*, which seems to have a quotation or the title of a subsequent work of art (play, film, book) in every line. Some romantic extracts from the plays (*Romeo and Juliet* and *Love's Labour's Lost*) have been included. Due to lack of space there was not room for more quotations.

The beloved (by convention, nearly always a woman) is always the centre of the Elizabethan love sonnet tradition. As Samuel Daniel puts it in his *Delia* sequence: '[a]ll my live's sweet consists in her alone' (sonnet 12), a sentiment found in most Elizabethan sonnet sequences and love poems. However, Daniel adds a final line: '[s]o much I love the most unloving one.' This is a typical Petrarchan-style (and Shakespearean) way to end a love sonnet, with a remark that can be construed as bitter and self-loathing as well as melancholy and yearning.

Writing about love can be almost as good as being in love, being *with* the beloved. Almost. Besides, the writing of love is the crucial aspect, which is why these people were poets, and why we know about their love experience. Millions of other people in love in the Elizabethan era did not write about it. The making of poetry is therefore the core activity, just as much as the kissing and arguments and the living of love. As Sidney says in the opening line of his sonnet 40 of *Astrophel and Stella*: '[a]s good to write as for to lie and groan'. Indeed, it is far better to write about one's experience instead of lying there suffering.

Sir Philip Sidney has to be thanked for much of Elizabethan love poetry, as much as Sir Thomas Wyatt, it seems, according to Michael Spiller. It was Sidney who wrote the first love sonnet sequence in English. His *Astrophel and Stella* created many of the rules of the game of writing sonnet sequences in the Petrarchan style. Sidney's beloved, Penelope Devereux, may have been not only the inspiration for Sidney's important sonnet sequence, but also for much of Elizabethan love poetry.[3] Sir Philip Sidney's work embodies many of the aspects of Elizabethan love poetry, and especially the sonnet sequence, of which *Astrophel and Stella* was the first. In Sidney's poetry we find the idealization of a beloved woman; the cultivation of the poetic self as an aristocratic, long-suffering lover; polished rhymes and structures; the use of vivid, sensual metaphors; Classical allusions; and the themes, usually given capital letters, of Time, Death, Hope, God, Love and Life. Sidney puts his finger on one of the self-conscious, self-reflexive aspects of love poetry when he writes in *Astrophel and Stella* (sonnet 5):

> It is most true, what we call *Cupid's* dart,
> An image is, which for ourselves we carve,
> And, fools, adore in temple of our heart...

Sidney knows that the love poem is a mirror into which the adoring poet gazes, like Narcissus, in love with his/ her own image-making. When Sidney writes in the first line of sonnet 106 – 'O absent presence *Stella* is not here' – he again pinpoints one of the fundamental situations of Elizabethan (and all) love poetry. The beloved is not there, but she is there: she is an 'absent presence'. She lingers in the poet's mind, embodying his (erotic) desire. All of the poetry flows from the fact that the beloved is not there, that he is an 'absent presence'.

For this edition, I have included more poems. A companion book, *Elizabethan Sonnets*, is published at the same time, as well as Elizabethan sonnet cycles by William Shakespeare (*Sonnets*), Michael Drayton (*Idea*), Samuel Daniel (*Delia*), Henry Constable (*Diana*), Edmund Spenser (*Amoretti*), and Sir Philip Sidney (*Astrophil and Stella*).

NOTES

1. Frances Yates, 1964. See also Frances Yates: *The Rosicrucian Enlightenment*, Routledge 1972; Ted Hughes: *Shakespeare and the Goddess of Complete Being*, Faber 1992; D.P. Walker: *Spiritual and Demonic Magic from Ficino to Campanella*, Warburg Institute 1958; Wayne Shumaker: *The Occult Sciences in the Renaissance*, University of California Press, Berkeley, California, 1972; Walter Pagel: *Paracelsus: An Introduction to Philosophical Medicine in the Era of the Renaissance*, Karger, New York 1958; Peter French: *John Dee*, Routledge 1972

2. Maureen Sabine: *Feminine Engendered Faith: The Poetry of John Donne and Richard Crashaw*, Macmillan 1992, 13

3. Penelope Devereux, Lady Rich (1563-1607), who was certainly responsible for the erotic fascination that produced Sir Philip Sidney's *Astrophel and Stella*, may also thereby have been responsible for the whole Elizabethan sonnet-sequence craze: for until she entered Sidney's life in the early months of 1581 neither he nor anyone else appears to have thought of writing a sequence of English sonnets in the Petrarchan style (Spiller, 1992, 102).

BIBLIOGRAPHY

Stevie Davies: *The Idea of Woman in Renaissance Literature: The Feminine Reclaimed*, Harvester Press, Brighton 1986

Maurice Evans, ed: *Elizabethan Sonnets*, Dent 1977

J.W. Lever: *The Elizabethan Love Sonnet,* London 1968

Michael R.G. Spiller: *The Development of the Sonnet: An Introduction*, Routledge 1992

Frances Yates, *Giordano Bruno and the Hermetic Tradition*, London 1964

ARTS, PAINTING, SCULPTURE

web: www.crmoon.com • e-mail: cresmopub@yahoo.co.uk

The Art of Andy Goldsworthy
Andy Goldsworthy: Touching Nature
Andy Goldsworthy in Close-Up
Andy Goldsworthy: Pocket Guide
Andy Goldsworthy In America
Land Art: A Complete Guide
The Art of Richard Long
Richard Long: Pocket Guide
Land Art In Great Britain
Land Art in Close-Up
Land Art In the U.S.A.
Land Art: Pocket Guide
Installation Art in Close-Up
Minimal Art and Artists In the 1960s and After
Colourfield Painting
Land Art DVD, TV documentary
Andy Goldsworthy DVD, TV documentary
The Erotic Object: Sexuality in Sculpture From Prehistory to the Present Day
Sex in Art: Pornography and Pleasure in Painting and Sculpture
Postwar Art
Sacred Gardens: The Garden in Myth, Religion and Art
Glorification: Religious Abstraction in Renaissance and 20th Century Art
Early Netherlandish Painting
Jasper Johns
Brice MardenLeonardo da Vinci
Piero della Francesca
Giovanni Bellini
Fra Angelico: Art and Religion in the Renaissance
Mark Rothko: The Art of Transcendence
Frank Stella: American Abstract Artist
Alison Wilding: The Embrace of Sculpture
Vincent van Gogh: Visionary Landscapes
Eric Gill: Nuptials of God
Constantin Brancusi: Sculpting the Essence of Things
Max Beckmann
Gustave Moreau
Caravaggio
Egon Schiele: Sex and Death In Purple Stockings
Delizioso Fotografico Fervore: Works In Process I
Sacro Cuore: Works In Process 2
The Light Eternal: J.M.W. Turner
The Madonna Glorified: Karen Arthurs

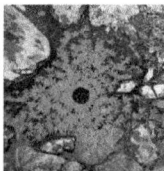

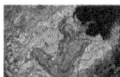

LITERATURE

J.R.R. Tolkien: The Books, The Films, The Whole Cultural Phenomenon
J.R.R. Tolkien: Pocket Guide
Beauties, Beasts and Enchantment: Classic French Fairy Tales
Tolkien's Heroic Quest
Brothers Grimm: German Popular Stories
Sexing Hardy: Thomas Hardy and Feminism
Thomas Hardy's Tess of the d'Urbervilles
Thomas Hardy's Jude the Obscure
Thomas Hardy: The Tragic Novels
Love and Tragedy: Thomas Hardy
The Poetry of Landscape in Hardy
Wessex Revisited: Thomas Hardy and John Cowper Powys
Wolfgang Iser: Essays and Interviews
Petrarch, Dante and the Troubadours
Maurice Sendak and the Art of Children's Book Illustration
Andrea Dworkin
Cixous, Irigaray, Kristeva: The Jouissance of French Feminism
Julia Kristeva: Art, Love, Melancholy, Philosophy, Semiotics and Psychoanalysis
Hélène Cixous I Love You: The Jouissance of Writing
Luce Irigaray: Lips, Kissing, and the Politics of Sexual Difference
Peter Redgrove: Here Comes the Flood
Peter Redgrove: Sex-Magic-Poetry-Cornwall
Lawrence Durrell: Between Love and Death, East and West
Love, Culture & Poetry: Lawrence Durrell
Cavafy: Anatomy of a Soul
German Romantic Poetry: Goethe, Novalis, Heine, Hölderlin
Novalis: Hymns To the Night
Feminism and Shakespeare
Shakespeare: The Sonnets
Shakespeare: Love, Poetry & Magic
The Passion of D.H. Lawrence
D.H. Lawrence: Symbolic Landscapes
D.H. Lawrence: Infinite Sensual Violence
The Ecstasies of John Cowper Powys
Sensualism and Mythology: The Wessex Novels of John Cowper Powys
Amorous Life: John Cowper Powys (H.W. Fawkner)
Postmodern Powys: New Essays on John Cowper Powys (Joe Boulter)
Rethinking Powys: Critical Essays on John Cowper Powys
Paul Bowles & Bernardo Bertolucci
Rainer Maria Rilke
Joseph Conrad: Heart of Darkness
In the Dim Void: Samuel Beckett
Samuel Beckett Goes into the Silence
André Gide: Fiction and Fervour
Jackie Collins and the Blockbuster Novel
Blinded By Her Light: The Love-Poetry of Robert Graves

POETRY

Ursula Le Guin: *Walking In Cornwall*
Peter Redgrove: Here Comes The Flood
Peter Redgrove: Sex-Magic-Poetry-Cornwall
Dante: Selections From the *Vita Nuova*
Petrarch, Dante and the Troubadours
William Shakespeare: *The Sonnets*
William Shakespeare: Complete Poems
Blinded By Her Light: The Love-Poetry of Robert Graves
Emily Dickinson: Selected Poems
Emily Brontë: Poems
Thomas Hardy: Selected Poems
Percy Bysshe Shelley: Poems
John Keats: Selected Poems
John Keats: Poems of 1820
D.H. Lawrence: Selected Poems
Edmund Spenser: Poems
Edmund Spenser: *Amoretti*
John Donne: Poems
Henry Vaughan: Poems
Sir Thomas Wyatt: Poems
Robert Herrick: Selected Poems
Rilke: Space, Essence and Angels in the Poetry of Rainer Maria Rilke
Rainer Maria Rilke: Selected Poems
Friedrich Hölderlin: Selected Poems
Arseny Tarkovsky: Selected Poems
Paul Verlaine: Selected Poems
Novalis: *Hymns To the Night*
Arthur Rimbaud: Selected Poems
Arthur Rimbaud: *A Season in Hell*
Arthur Rimbaud and the Magic of Poetry
D.J. Enright: By-Blows
Jeremy Reed: *Brigitte's Blue Heart*
Jeremy Reed: *Claudia Schiffer's Red Shoes*
Gorgeous Little Orpheus
Radiance: New Poems
Crescent Moon Book of Nature Poetry
Crescent Moon Book of Love Poetry
Crescent Moon Book of Mystical Poetry
Crescent Moon Book of Elizabethan Love Poetry
Crescent Moon Book of Metaphysical Poetry
Crescent Moon Book of Romantic Poetry
Pagan America: New American Poetry

MEDIA, CINEMA, FEMINISM and CULTURAL STUDIES

J.R.R. Tolkien: The Books, The Films, The Whole Cultural Phenomenon
J.R.R. Tolkien: Pocket Guide
The *Lord of the Rings* Movies: Pocket Guide
The Ghost Dance: The Origins of Religion
The Cinema of Hayao Miyazaki
Hayao Miyazaki: *Princess Mononoke*: Pocket Movie Guide
Hayao Miyazaki: *Spirited Away*: Pocket Movie Guide
The Peyote Cult
HomeGround: The Kate Bush Anthology
Tim Burton : Hallowe'en For Hollywood
Ken Russell
Cixous, Irigaray, Kristeva: The *Jouissance* of French Feminism
Julia Kristeva: Art, Love, Melancholy, Philosophy, Semiotics and Psychoanalysis
Luce Irigaray: Lips, Kissing, and the Politics of Sexual Difference
Hélene Cixous I Love You: The *Jouissance* of Writing
Andrea Dworkin
'Cosmo Woman': The World of Women's Magazines
Women in Pop Music
Discovering the Goddess (Geoffrey Ashe)
The Poetry of Cinema
The Sacred Cinema of Andrei Tarkovsky
Andrei Tarkovsky: Pocket Guide
Andrei Tarkovsky: *Mirror*: Pocket Movie Guide
Walerian Borowczyk: Cinema of Erotic Dreams
Jean-Luc Godard: The Passion of Cinema
Jean-Luc Godard: Pocket Guide
John Hughes and Eighties Cinema
Ferris Buller's Day Off: Pocket Movie Guide
The Cinema of Richard Linklater
Liv Tyler: Star In Ascendance
Blade Runner and the Films of Philip K. Dick
Paul Bowles and Bernardo Bertolucci
Media Hell: Radio, TV and the Press
Detonation Britain: Nuclear War in the UK
Feminism and Shakespeare
Wild Zones: Pornography, Art and Feminism
Sex in Art: Pornography and Pleasure in Painting and Sculpture
Sexing Hardy: Thomas Hardy and Feminism

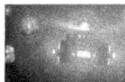

*The Light Eternal is a model monograph, an exemplary job. The subject matter of the book is
beautifully organised and dead on beam. (Lawrence Durrell)*
It is amazing for me to see my work treated with such passion and respect. (Andrea Dworkin)
Sex-Magic-Poetry-Cornwall is a very rich essay... It is like a brightly-lighted box. (Peter Redgrove)

CRESCENT MOON PUBLISHING   P.O. Box 1312, Maidstone, Kent, ME14 5XU, Great Britain
0044-1622-729593   cresmopub@yahoo.co.uk   www.crmoon.com